RIGHT AND WRONG

By the same author:

A Dictionary of Non-Christian Religions (Hulton)
A Book of World Religions (Hulton)
The World's Living Religions (Pan)
What World Religions Teach (Harrap)
Avatar and Incarnation (Faber & Faber)
Jesus in the Qur'an (Faber & Faber)
Upanishads, Gita and Bible (Harper)
Religion in Africa (Penguin)
Witchcraft European and African (Faber & Faber)
The Indestructible Soul (Allen & Unwin)

THEMES FOR LIVING

A Source Book selected from Religious and Ethical
Writings of the World

by

Geoffrey Parrinder

Professor of the Comparative Study of Religions,
University of London

Book II

RIGHT AND WRONG

Hulton Educational Publications

First published 1973 by Hulton Educational Publications Ltd.,
Raans Road, Amersham, Bucks.

Printed in Great Britain by Cox & Wyman Ltd.,
London, Reading and Fakenham

FOREWORD

The source book, of which this is a part, offers a collection of passages chosen from many ages and countries, to illustrate some of the major themes and principles of moral living. Such teachings are innumerable, and sometimes the choice may indicate personal preference or easy accessibility. No anthology could possibly contain all the interesting texts on these subjects, which might include most of Plato, the Bible, the Qur'an, the Bhagavad Gita, and the Chinese Classics, at the least. But the great interest that is taken today in the religions and philosophies of the east, the many texts that are available as never before, and the possibility that this book may be used to illustrate courses in comparative religion and ethics, have led to selections being made regularly from the major religions and cultures.

The subjects are arranged according to themes, and within most of them passages are chosen from the great religions and civilizations. Some of these are isolated texts in a mass of material, or they occur among verses of uneven value, but they represent viewpoints expressed in those cultures. With some exceptions, selections generally proceed on each topic from classical Europe, the Bible, the Qur'an, the Indian scriptures, the Chinese classics, and modern writers. By cross reference to the lists of contents, teachings of a particular religion and culture can be followed through.

There are four books, or parts, in this anthology, which treat broadly of Man and God, Right and Wrong, Society, and the Goal of Life. The four books may be studied individually, but it may be advisable to take note of the unity of the four books, and observe that themes in one part have relevance to themes in another. Most selections are prefaced with a sentence or two of introduction, and the known or approximate date of each author or writing is given on its first occurrence in the set of four parts. These dates are also roughly indicated in the Time Chart in each part. Bibliography and Index follow the fourth part. Suggestions are given after each chapter for discussion, and readers can pick up these points and enlarge the discussion by looking for other passages not quoted in the text. Some of these may be found in modern writings, since the selections given in this book are principally from ancient times, as basic to religions and philosophies, and only a few quotations have been possible from the present century because of the mass of material.

It is hoped that this work will be helpful in moral and religious education, school and college assemblies, in class study and for private interest. Perhaps these hundreds of passages will reveal the close association of morals with faith and ideology. In the words of Dr. S. Radhakrishnan, former President of India, in the preface to his translation of the Dhammapada, 'the tree of civilization has its roots in spiritual values which most of us do not recognize. Without these roots the leaves would have fallen and left the tree a lifeless stump.'

The author thanks the following for allowing him to quote from the works mentioned: George Allen & Unwin Ltd.: 'Mahatma Gandhi's Ideas' by C. F. Andrews. The Longman Group Ltd.: 'The African Past' by B. Davidson. Cambridge University Press: 'Rabi'a the Mystic' by M. Smith. The Hutchinson Publishing Group Ltd.: 'Manual of Zen Buddhism' trs. by D. T. Suzuki. Columbia University Press: 'Sources of Chinese Tradition', ed. W. T. de Bary. Collier-Macmillan Publishers: 'The Great Asian Religions' by W. W. Chan.

BOOK II

RIGHT AND WRONG

The right and best ways of living have been discussed for many centuries, in codes of law and lists of virtues. These vary from place to place, and time to time, though beneath regional differences there is always a concern for private and public good. The special virtues which are cherished, as well as the vices that are condemned, throw light on the character of a civilization.

This is a selection, from many formulations of law and morality, and readers can find others to compare with those that are collected here, and then their teachings may be considered and evaluated.

CONTENTS

III. SPECIAL VIRTUES

IV. HAPPINESS

I

CODES OF BEHAVIOUR

Lists of commandments and virtues have been formulated from ancient times. Some of the early ones influenced later ideals, both in the ways in which they agree and disagree with them.

1. Babylonian Laws (Hammurabi)

The Code of Hammurabi, who ruled Babylon from about 1728 to 1686 B.C., is one of the most ancient and famous statements of social morality. It was discovered in 1902, inscribed on a stone pillar or stela containing 282 clauses. It is far too long to quote in full, but some of the laws may be compared with other ancient commandments. The penalties of wrongdoing were harsh, but were probably the maximum prescribed. Hammurabi regarded himself as the shepherd of his people, a task entrusted to him by Marduk, the god of the Babylonian empire. The second law prescribes an ordeal, where the river is a god which gives judgement.

When Marduk commanded me to guide the people rightly and to direct the land, I established law and justice in the language of the land in order to promote the welfare of the people. Then I decreed:

1. If a man accuses another man and brings a charge of murder against him, but does not prove it, his accuser shall be put to death.

2. If a man accuses another of laying a spell upon him, but has not proved it, the accused shall go to the sacred river. He shall plunge into the sacred river, and if the river overpowers him, his accuser shall take possession of his estate. If the sacred river

shows his innocence, and he comes out safely, his accuser shall be put to death, and he that plunged into the sacred river shall take over the estate of him that accused him.

3. If a man has borne false witness in a trial, and has not proved the statement that he made, if that case is a capital trial, that man shall be put to death.

4. If he has borne false witness in a civil law case, he shall pay the damages in that suit . . .

8. If a man has stolen an ox, or a sheep, or an ass, or a pig, or a boat, whether from a temple or from the state, he shall pay thirtyfold. If it belonged to a commoner, he shall return tenfold. If the thief cannot pay, he shall be put to death . . .

129. If a man's wife is caught lying with another, they shall be bound and thrown into the water. If the woman's husband wishes to spare his wife, then the king may also spare his subject . . .

195. If a son has struck his father, his hand shall be cut off.

196. If a man has knocked out the eye of a noble, his eye shall be knocked out.

197. If he had broken the limb of a noble, his limb shall be broken.

198. If he has knocked out the eye of a commoner, he shall pay a piece of silver . . .

These are the laws of justice set up by Hammurabi, the efficient king, and through which he brought firm guidance and good government to the land.

2. Ten Commandments (Exodus)

This code of law was said to have been spoken by God and told to the Hebrew people by Moses, perhaps about 1300 B.C. The first four commandments give duties to God and the last six duties to men.

I am the Lord your God, who brought you out of the land of Egypt, out of the house of bondage.

You shall have no other gods before me.

You shall not make for yourself a carved image, or any likeness of anything that is in heaven above, or in the earth beneath, or in the water under the earth. You shall not bow down to them, or serve them. For I the Lord your God am a jealous God, visiting the iniquity of the fathers upon the children to the third and fourth generation of those who hate me, but showing mercy to thousands of those who love me and keep my commandments.

You shall not take the name of the Lord your God in vain; for the Lord will not hold him guiltless who takes his name in vain.

Remember the sabbath day, to keep it holy. Six days you shall labour and do all your work, but the seventh day is a sabbath to the Lord your God. In it you shall not do any work; you, or your son, or your daughter, your manservant, or your maidservant, or your cattle, or the stranger who is within your gates. For in six days the Lord made heaven and earth, the sea, and all that is in them, and rested the seventh day. Therefore the Lord blessed the sabbath day and made it holy.

Honour your father and mother, that your days may be long in the land which the Lord your God gives you.

You shall not kill.

You shall not commit adultery.

You shall not steal.

You shall not bear false witness against your neighbour.

You shall not covet your neighbour's house, you shall not covet your neighbour's wife, or his manservant, or his maidservant, or his ox, or his ass, or anything that is your neighbour's.

(Exodus 20, 2–17; Deuteronomy 5, 6–21)

3. Summary of the Law (Jesus)

In reply to a question Jesus, in the first century A.D., *indicated two laws as most important. The first was from Deuteronomy 6, 4–5, the Hebrew confession of faith, and the second was taken from Leviticus 19, 18.*

One of the scribes came, and heard them questioning together, and seeing that he answered them well, asked him: Which commandment is the first of all?

Jesus answered; The first is, Hear, O Israel, the Lord our God, the Lord is one; and you shall love the Lord your God with all your heart, and with all your soul, and with all your mind, and with all your strength.

The second is this; You shall love your neighbour as yourself.

There is no other commandment greater than these.

And the scribe said to him: Truly, Master, you have rightly said that he is one, and there is no other but he. And to love him with all the heart, and with all the understanding, and with all the strength, and to love one's neighbour as oneself, is much more than all whole burnt offerings and sacrifices.

(Mark 12, 28–33)

4. **Serve God and do Good** (Qur'an)

The Qur'an is taken by Muslims as the words of God delivered through the Prophet Muhammad (A.D. 570–632). A summary combines duty to God and man.

Do not associate another god with God, lest you are despised and forsaken. Your Lord has decreed that you shall not serve any but him.

Do good to your parents. If either or both of them attain to old age with you, do not say 'Fie' to them, or scold them but speak respectfully.

Bear yourself humbly to them in compassion and say:

My Lord, have mercy on them as they brought me up when I was young. Your Lord knows what is in your minds. If you are righteous, he is forgiving to those who turn to him.

Give the kinsman his due, and the needy, and the follower of the way, and do not squander wastefully . . .

Do not kill your children for fear of poverty. We provide for them and for you, and killing them is a great sin.

Avoid immorality, which is indecent and its way is evil . . .

Do not take the property of an orphan . . .

Give full measure and weigh with just balances . . .

Do not walk boisterously upon the earth . . .

This is some of the wisdom which your Lord has revealed.

(Qur'an 17, 23–41/22–39. The first verse reference is a European numbering, the second an Islamic numbering)

5. Laws for Different Classes (Manu)

The Code or Institutes of Manu is a pre-Christian Indian collection of mythology and social regulations ascribed to a legendary Manu or 'thinking' man. The self-existent God is credited with giving regulations to four classes or castes of men: Brahmin priests, Kshatriya warrior-rulers, Vaishya farmer-merchants, and Shudra servants.

In order to protect this world he, the resplendent one, assigned separate occupations to those who sprang from his mouth, arms, thighs and feet.

To priests he assigned teaching and study, sacrificing for their own benefit and for others, giving and accepting of alms.

To rulers he commanded to protect the people, to bestow gifts, to offer sacrifices, to study, and to abstain from attachment to sensual pleasures.

To merchants to tend cattle, to bestow gifts, to offer sacrifices, to study, to trade, to lend money, and to cultivate land.

The Lord prescribed only one duty to serfs, to serve the other three classes meekly.

(Laws of Manu 1, 87–91)

6. Noble Eightfold Path (Buddha)

Gautama the Buddha, the 'enlightened one', about 560–480 B.C. or somewhat later, taught a Middle Way between the extremes of sensuality and asceticism. This was the Noble Eightfold Path, a succession of actions each termed 'right', beginning with the view of the truth, resolve to follow it, proper speech, action and meditation. The Noble Eightfold Path is also the last of the Four Noble Truths (see Book IV, 11).

The Buddha has gained knowledge of the Middle Way, which gives insight and wisdom, and leads to calm, perception, enlightenment and Nirvana.

What is the Middle Way which gives insight? . . .

It is the Noble Eightfold Path, namely, Right Views, Right Resolve, Right Speech, Right Action, Right Pursuits, Right Effort, Right Mindfulness, Right Concentration.

(From Turning the Wheel of Doctrine, Samyutta Nikaya 420, etc.)

7. Five Precepts and Ten Rules (Vinaya)

To the Buddha are attributed five moral rules (Pancha Sila or Pansil), which are enjoined on laymen and monks alike. A further five are enjoined on monks.

I enjoin ten rules for novices:
Refrain from taking life.
Refrain from taking what is not given.
Refrain from immorality.
Refrain from false speech.
Refrain from liquors which cause carelessness.

Refrain from untimely food.
Refrain from dancing, singing, music and seeing shows.
Refrain from the use of garlands, scents and ointments for
     adornment.
Refrain from a large or high bed.
Refrain from accepting gold or silver.

(Book of Discipline, Vinaya, Mahavagga 1, 56)

8. **Edicts for Men and Animals** (Ashoka)

Ashoka ruled much of India from 273 to 232 B.C., became a Buddhist, and was one of the most humane kings of history.

No living thing may be killed for sacrifice . . .

Everywhere medical services have been provided in two kinds. These are for the medical care of men and the medical care of animals. Medicinal herbs, useful to men and beasts, have been imported and planted wherever they did not grow. Roots too and fruits have been imported and planted wherever they did not grow. Wells have been dug along the roads and trees planted for the benefit of men and animals . . .

You have been set over many thousands of living beings, so that you may gain the affection of men. All men are my children, and just as I desire for my children that they should enjoy prosperity and happiness in this world and the next, so also I desire the same for all men. But you do not grasp the full extent of this truth, and if perhaps one among you does grasp it, that is only in part and not wholly. So consider this well even if you are well off yourselves.

A man may suffer imprisonment or torture, and then is released without reason and many people suffer further. Then you must desire to be impartial. But this cannot be practised by men who have certain faults, namely: envy, short temper, harshness, impatience, obstinacy, idleness or slackness. You must try to avoid such faults.

(From First Major Rock Edict, Second Major Rock Edict, Provincials' Edict)

9. **Duty and Goodness** (Confucius)

Confucius lived in China 551–479 B.C.

The Master said: Let a young man behave well to his parents at home and to his elders abroad. Let him be circumspect and truthful, and while showing kindly feelings to all men seek the company of the Good.

Having done so, if he has energy to spare, let him study the polite arts . . .

How can a man be considered wise, if he is free to choose but does not prefer to dwell with the Good?

The Master said: A man cannot long endure adversity, or long enjoy prosperity, without goodness. The good man is content with goodness, but the merely wise man only covets it . . .

The Master said: The man who has really set his heart on goodness will dislike no one.

(Analects 1, 6; 4, 1–4)

10. The Silent Way of Recompense
(Chou Meng-yen)

Much of Chinese popular religion was inspired by Taoism, which sought to follow the Way (Tao) of heaven and earth by quietness. The text of the Silent Way of Recompense was attributed to a Taoist deity and dates from medieval times or earlier, copies being found in most villages and distributed by goodwill organizations.

I have extensively practised the Silent Way of Recompense . . .

Whoever wants to expand his field of happiness, let him rely on his moral nature.

Do good work at all times, and practise in secret meritorious deeds of all kinds.

Benefit living creatures and human beings. Cultivate goodness and happiness.

Be honest and straight and, on behalf of Heaven, promote moral reform. Be compassionate and merciful and, for the sake of the country, save the people.

Be loyal to your ruler and filial to your parents.

Be respectful towards elders and truthful to friends . . .

Help people in distress as you would help a fish in a dried-up rut. Free people from danger as you would free a sparrow from a fine net.

Be compassionate to orphans and kind to widows. Respect the aged and have pity on the poor.

Collect food and clothing and relieve those who are hungry and cold along the road.

(From Chou Meng-yen (ed.), Yin-chih wen kuang-i)

11. Seventeen Articles (Shotoku)

Prince Shotoku ruled Japan from A.D. 573 to 621, supported Buddhism, and was also deeply read in the moral and administrative teachings of Confucianism, so that his Articles show the influence of Confucian ethical and political doctrines. They are too long to print here, and the first sentence of each is given.

Harmony is to be valued and an avoidance of wanton opposition to be honoured.

Sincerely reverence the three treasures: the Buddha, the Doctrine, and the Order.

When you receive imperial commands, fail not scrupulously to obey them.

Ministers and functionaries should make decorous behaviour their leading principle.

Ceasing from gluttony and abandoning covetous desires, deal impartially with the suits which are submitted to you.

Chastise that which is evil and encourage that which is good. This was the excellent rule of antiquity.

Let every man have his own charge and let not the spheres of duty be confused.

Let ministers and functionaries attend court early in the morning and retire late.

Good faith is the foundation of right.

Let us cease from wrath and refrain from angry looks.

Give clear appreciation to merit and demerit.

Let not the provincial authorities ... levy exaction on the people.

Let all persons entrusted with office attend equally to their functions.

Ministers and functionaries, be not envious.

Turn away from that which is private and set your faces towards that which is public.

Let the people be employed at seasonable times.

Decisions on important matters should not be made by one person alone.

(Adapted from W. G. Aston, Nihongi 2, 128–133)

12. **Baha'i Commands** (Abdu'l Baha)

Abdu'l Baha (Abbas Effendi), 'the servant of glory', 1844–1921, a leader of the Baha'i community, founded by Baha'u'llah, gave instructions to his followers in America, of which the first clauses are given here.

To live the life.
To be no cause of grief to anyone.
To love each other fully.
To be kind to all people and to love them with a pure spirit.

Should opposition or injury happen, we must bear it and be kind, and, through all, we must love the people.

Should calamity exist in the greatest degree, we must rejoice, for these things are the gifts and favours of God.

To be silent concerning the faults of others; to pray for them; and help them, through kindness, to correct their faults.

To look always at the good and not at the bad. If a man has ten good qualities and one bad one, we must look at the ten and forget the one. And if a man has ten bad qualities and one good one, we must look at the one and forget the ten.

To never allow ourselves to speak one unkind word about another; even though that other be our enemy. To rebuke those who speak to us of the faults of others.

All our deeds must be done in kindness.

(The Splendour of God, p. 122f.)

13. **Rules of Soul-force** (Gandhi)

M. K. Gandhi, the Indian leader (1869–1948), gave these rules for his Ashrams or retreat-centres of Soul-force. Only the headings are given here.

Our Scriptures have laid down certain rules as maxims of human life. They tell us that without living according to these maxims we are incapable of having a reasonable perception of Religion . . . The following are the rules that have been drawn up and have to be observed by everyone who seeks to be a member.

The first and foremost is: the Vow of Truth.

Then we come to: the Doctrine of Non-violence,
the Vow of Celibacy [chastity],
the Vow of the Control of the Palate,
the Vow of Non-thieving,
the Vow of Home Support,
the Vow of Fearlessness,
the Vow of Freeing Untouchables,
the Vow of Education through the Vernacular,
the Vow of Manual Work,
the Vow of the Religious Use of Politics.

(MS statement, see Mahatma Gandhi's Ideas, p. 102ff.)

Discussion

Compare the Code of Hammurabi with the Ten Commandments.

Why is love towards God the first commandment?

Refrain from taking life. What does this imply?

How can a man be considered wise if he does not dwell with the good?

Good faith is the foundation of right (Shotoku). Discuss.

Look always at the good and not at the bad. Discuss.

Different countries and teachers have different views. Does this mean that one opinion is as good as another, or that only one is right and the others are all wrong?

II

VIRTUES

There are many different lists and descriptions of the basic virtues. Plato (429–347 B.C.) spoke of justice and piety, self-control and courage. Then he added wisdom, and this came to dominate. Four cardinal virtues were enumerated: wisdom, self-control (temperance), justice and courage. Wisdom was set above and ahead of the other virtues.

14. Four Cardinal Virtues (Plato)

Virtue is not to be bought by bartering pleasure for pleasure, and pain for pain, and fear for fear, and the greater for the less, like coins. There is only one sterling coin for which all these things ought to be exchanged, and that is wisdom. All that is bought and sold for this, whether courage or self-control or justice, is real. In a word, true virtue cannot be without wisdom, and it matters nothing whether pleasure, and fear, and all other such things, are present or absent. But I think that the virtue which is composed of pleasures and fears bartered with one another, and severed from true wisdom, is only a shadow of true virtue, and that it has no freedom, nor health, nor truth. True virtue, in reality, is a kind of purifying from all these things; and self-control, and justice, and courage, and wisdom itself, are the purification.

(Phaedo 69)

15. Theory and Practice (Cicero, 106–43 B.C.)

The whole subject of duties, in its greatest latitude, comprehends under it these two parts: the first is taken up in ex-

plaining what is good, and what our greatest good. The second is
in certain directions and precepts, according to which on all
occasions it is our duty to govern our lives and actions. To the
first part belong such questions as these: whether all duties are
perfect or not? and whether one can be greater or less than
another? with several others to the same purpose. Not but that
the duties of this second part, the rules and precepts of which are
laid down, have some tendency and relation to our chief good;
but only it does not so plainly appear, because they seem to
concern more immediately the government of our lives and regu-
lation of our manners.

(Offices I, 3)

16. Three Theological Virtues (Paul)

*Christian theologians, like Augustine of Hippo (354–430), took over
the four Cardinal or Natural Virtues of Plato and Aristotle and con-
trasted them with the three 'theological' or scriptural virtues of Faith,
Hope and Charity, given by Paul. The translation 'love' is more true
to Paul's meaning than 'charity' in modern English.*

Though I speak with the tongues of men and of angels, and
have not love, I am become as sounding brass or a tinkling
cymbal. And though I have the gift of prophecy, and understand
all mysteries, and all knowledge; and though I have all faith, so
that I could remove mountains, and have not love, I am nothing.
And though I bestow all my goods to feed the poor, and though I
give my body to be burned, and have not love, it profits me
nothing. Love suffers long and is kind; love does not envy, does
not boast, is not puffed up, does not behave unseemly, seeks not
its own, is not provoked, thinks no evil, does not rejoice in evil
but rejoices in the truth. Love bears all things, believes all
things, hopes all things, endures all things. Love never fails ...
and now faith, hope and love abide, these three; but the greatest
of these is love.

(I Corinthians 13)

17. Three Virtues – Da, Da, Da (Upanishads)

Three cardinal virtues are given in a parable in the Hindu Up-
anishads where Praja-pati, 'lord of creatures', instructs gods, men and
demons. To each he says Da, which each interprets respectively as
Damyata, 'restrain yourselves', Datta, 'give', and Dayadhvam, 'be
compassionate'. These three are a model for men. The passage has
become known in the West as it ends T. S. Eliot's poem, 'The Waste
Land', the section beginning 'then spoke the thunder', and ending
with threefold Shantih, 'peace'.

The threefold offspring of Prajapati – gods, men and demons,
lived with their father as students of sacred knowledge.

After they had stayed with him as students the gods said:
'Speak to us, sir.' He spoke one word, 'Da. Did you understand?'
They said, 'We did understand, you said to us, Restrain your-
selves.' 'Yes,' he said, 'you did understand.'

Then the men said to him, 'Speak to us, sir.' He spoke one
word, 'Da. Did you understand?' They said, 'We did understand, you said to us, Give.' 'Yes,' he said, 'you did understand.'

Then the demons said to him, 'Speak to us, sir.' He spoke one
word, 'Da. Did you understand?' They said, 'We did under-
sand. You said to us, Be compassionate.' 'Yes,' he said, 'you did
understand.'

This is what the divine voice, the thunder, repeats: Da-Da-
Da: restrain yourselves, give, be compassionate. You should
practise this threefold lesson: restraint, giving, and compassion.

(Brihad-aranyaka Upanishad 5, 2)

18. Four Great Vows (Buddhist)

These vows are recited after every service of Zen ('meditation') and other Buddhists. They are vows of Bodhi-sattvas, 'beings of enlightenment', dedicated to serve all beings.

However innumerable beings are, I vow to save them;
However inexhaustible the passions are, I vow to extinguish them;
However immeasurable the Teachings are, I vow to master them;
However incomparable the Buddha-truth is, I vow to attain it.

(D. T. Suzuki, Manual of Zen Buddhism, p. 14)

19. Eight Parts of Yoga (Patanjali)

Patanjali in India, perhaps about the beginning of the Christian era, taught a system of Yoga, 'discipline', of mind, body, behaviour and meditation. Here he sketches meditation which depends on self-control.

On the destruction of impurity by the practice of the parts of Yoga, there comes enlightenment leading up to discriminative knowledge.

The eight parts of Yoga are: self-control, rules regulating life, bodily posture, breath-control, withdrawal of the senses from objects, fixed attention, meditation and concentration.

The self-controls are: non-violence, truth, honesty, chastity and abstinence.

These are a Great Vow, universal, and unlimited by class, place, time or circumstance.

(Yoga Sutras 2, 28–31)

20. Five Virtues (Confucius)

Confucius said: He who could practise the Five Virtues everywhere under Heaven would be good.

Tzu Chang [a disciple] begged to know what these were.

Confucius said: Courtesy, magnanimity, good faith, diligence,
and kindness.

He who is courteous is not scorned,
he who is magnanimous wins the multitude,
he who is of good faith is trusted by the people,
he who is diligent succeeds in all he undertakes,
he who is kind can get service from the people.

(Analects 17, 6)

21. Four Others (Mencius, fourth century B.C.)

No man is without a feeling of compassion, or a feeling of shame,
or a feeling of consideration for others, or a feeling of plain right
and wrong...

Let a man but attend to expanding and developing these four
elements in his being, and his progress will burst out like a newly
kindled fire or a spring from the ground. If these virtues can be
fully developed, they are strong enough to safeguard all within
the four seas. If they are allowed to remain undeveloped, they
will not be enough even for the service due to one's parents.

(Mencius 2, A, 6)

22. **Three Treasures** (Tao Te Ching, third century B.C.)

I have three treasures, to guard and keep.

The first is pity, the second is frugality, the third is refusal to be foremost in the world.

Only he that pities can afford to be brave.

Only he that is frugal can be profuse.

Only he that refuses to be foremost in all things is able to be chief of ministers.

To forsake pity for bravery, to forsake frugality for expansion, to forsake the rear for the front, this is death.

Through pity one will conquer, and will guard without defence. What heaven helps, it protects with the gift of pity.

(Tao Te Ching 67)

23. **Wisdom, Characters, Tempers** (Mishnah)

The Mishnah, from a root meaning 'to repeat', is a collection of ancient Hebrew teachings on ritual and conduct. Part of it, the Ethics of the Fathers, is included in the Hebrew prayer book.

There are seven marks of an uncultured man, and seven of a wise man.

The wise man does not speak before him who is greater than he in wisdom; and does not break in upon the speech of his fellow; he is not hasty to answer; he questions according to the subject matter, and answers to the point; he speaks upon the first thing first, and the last last; regarding that which he has not understood he says, I do not understand it, and he acknowledges the truth.

The reverse of all this is to be found in an uncultured man . . .

There are four characters among men:

He who says, What is mine is mine and what is thine is thine, his is a neutral character; some say, this is a character like that of Sodom.

He who says, What is mine is thine and what is thine is mine, is a boor.

He who says, What is mine is thine and what is thine is thine, is a saint.

He who says, What is thine is mine and what is mine is mine, is a wicked man.

There are four kinds of tempers:

He whom it is easy to provoke and easy to pacify, his loss disappears in his gain.

He whom it is hard to provoke and hard to pacify, his gain disappears in his loss.

He whom it is hard to provoke and easy to pacify, is a saint.

He whom it is easy to provoke and hard to pacify, is a wicked man.

(Ethics of the Fathers 5, 10, 13–14)

24. African Qualities (Ibn Battuta)

The absence of written texts from ancient Africa means that most traditions have gone unrecorded. But in the fourteenth century a Berber traveller, Ibn Battuta (1304–77), visited much of Africa and Asia and wrote down his impressions. Here he writes of the empire of Mali in West Africa.

Among the admirable qualities of these people, the following may be noted:

1. The small number of acts of injustice that one finds there; for the Negroes are of all people those who most abhor injustice. The sultan pardons no one who is guilty of it.

2. The complete and general safety one enjoys throughout the land. The traveller has no more reason than the man who stays at home to fear brigands, thieves or ravishers.

3. The blacks do not confiscate the goods of white men [Berbers] who die in their country, not even when these consist of big treasures. They deposit them, on the contrary, with a man of confidence among the whites until those who have a right to the goods present themselves and take possession.

4. They make their prayers punctually, and assiduously attend their meetings of the faithful.

(Ibn Battuta, Travels, trs. B. Davidson, The African Past p. 90)

25. Arunta Generosity (Spencer and Gillen)

A standard work on the Arunta or Aranda tribes of central Australia in 1899 discussed some of their characteristics.

Generosity is certainly one of his leading features. He is always accustomed to give a share of his food, or of what he may possess, to his fellows. It may be, of course, objected to this that in so doing he is only following an old-established custom, the breaking of which would expose him to harsh treatment and to being looked upon as a churlish fellow. It will, however, hardly be denied that, as this custom expresses the idea that in this particular matter every one is supposed to act in a kindly way towards certain individuals, the very existence of such a custom, even if it be carried out in the hope of securing at some time a *quid pro quo*, shows that the native is alive to the fact that an action which benefits some one else is worthy of being performed.

And here we may notice a criticism frequently made with regard to the native, and that is that he is incapable of gratitude. It is undoubtedly true that the native is not in the habit of showing anything like excessive gratitude on receiving gifts from the white man, but then neither does he think it necessary to express his gratitude when he receives a gift from one of his own tribe ... It is with him a fixed habit to give away part of what he has ... giving and receiving are matters of course in everyday life ...

With regard to their treatment of one another it may be said that this is marked on the whole by considerable kindness ... The women are certainly not treated usually with anything which could be called excessive harshness. They have, as amongst other savage tribes, to do a considerable part, but by no means all, of the work of the camp, but, after all, in a good season this does not amount to very much, and in a bad season men and women suffer alike, and of what there is they get their share. (*B. Spencer and F. J. Gillen, The Native Tribes of Central Australia, p. 48f.*)

26. American Indian Morality (Catlin)

Early Europeans in America often spoke of the Indians as savages, heathens, and worse. A different opinion was expressed by George Catlin who from his home in Wyoming travelled for eight years, from 1832–39, to some of the wildest parts of North America.

I fearlessly assert to the world, and I defy contradiction, that the North American Indian is everywhere, in his native state, a highly moral and religious being, endowed by his Maker with an intuitive knowledge of some great Author of his being, and the Universe; in dread of whose displeasure he constantly lives, with the apprehension before him of a future state, where he expects to be rewarded or punished according to the merits he has gained in this world.

I have made this a subject of unceasing enquiry during all my travels, and from every individual Indian with whom I have conversed on the subject, from the highest to the lowest and most pitiably ignorant, I have received evidence enough, as well as from their numerous and humble modes of worship, to convince the mind . . .

Morality and virtue, I venture to say, the civilized world need not undertake to teach them . . . To each other I have found these people kind and honourable, and endowed with every feeling of parental, of filial, and conjugal affection, that is met in more enlightened communities. I have found them moral and religious: and I am bound to give them credit for their zeal, which is often exhibited in their modes of worship, however insufficient they may seem to us, or may be in the estimation of the Great Spirit . . . I am bound to say that I never saw any other people of any colour, who spend so much of their lives in humbling themselves before, and worshipping the Great Spirit, as some of these tribes do.

(*G. Catlin, Letters and Notes on the Manners, Customs and Condition of the North American Indians, vol. 2, p. 242–3*)

27. Virtue as the Mean (Aristotle)

Aristotle (384–322 B.C.*) taught that virtue is a relative Mean or Middle Way between extremes, and he gave a list of virtues with their opposite extremes to illustrate his doctrine. It was not always easy to apply and Aristotle admitted that sometimes it does not hold; there is no mean in adultery. But his Mean was intended to be in itself an extreme, that is to say that in value it is a peak, surpassing all other ways.*

Virtue is concerned with feelings and actions, in which the excess is wrong and the defect is blamed, but the mean is praised and goes right, and both these circumstances belong to Virtue. Virtue then is in a sense a mean state, since it certainly has an aptitude for aiming at the mean.

One may go wrong in many different ways, but right only in one ... it is easy to miss the mark, but hard to hit it. For these reasons, therefore, both the excess and defect belong to Vice, and the mean state to Virtue ...

Virtue then is 'a state apt to exercise deliberate choice, being in the relative mean, determined by reason, and as a man of practical wisdom would determine'. . .

1. In respect of fears and confidence or boldness: the Mean state is Courage; men may exceed ... in rashness; or the man who has too much fear and too little confidence is called a coward.

2. In respect of pleasures and pains (but not all, and perhaps fewer pains than pleasures); the Mean state here is perfected Self-Mastery; the defect total absence of self-control ...

3. In respect of giving and taking wealth (a): the mean state is Liberality; the excess Prodigality, the defect Stinginess ...

4. In respect of wealth (b) ... a mean state called Munificence ... the excess called by the names either of Want of taste or Vulgar profusion, and the defect Paltriness ...

5. In respect of honour and dishonour (a): the mean state Greatness of Soul, the excess which may be called Boasting, and the defect Littleness of soul.

6. In respect of honour and dishonour (b): there is a state
bearing the same relation to Greatness of Soul as we said just
now Liberality does to Munificence, with the difference that is of
being about a small amount of the same thing . . .

7. In respect of anger . . . we will call the mean state Meekness
. . . and of the extremes, let the man who is excessive be named
Passionate, and the faulty state Passionateness, and him who is
deficient Angerless, and the defect Angerlessness.

(Ethics 2, 1106–8)

28. The Confucian Mean (Tzu Ssu)

*Moderation in conduct was the mark of the Chinese Gentleman (see
Book I, 72), who was one who avoided extremes like Confucius
himself. An essay on the Mean, from the Book of Rites, has, along
with the Great Learning, the Analects and Mencius (Book I, 62),
formed the basis of classical Chinese education. The Mean is ascribed
to Tzu Ssu (483–402 B.C.?), or other writers, and it may include
much later texts. The Chinese title of the essay Chung Yung, combines the elements of 'centrality' and 'normality', and suggests the
ideas of moderation and balance.*

When the passions, such as pleasure and anger and sorrow
and joy, have not awakened, the state is called that of centrality.
When these passions awaken and each and all attain due measure
and degree, it is called the state of harmony.

The state of centrality is the great root, and the state of harmony is the far-reaching Way of all existence in the world.

Once centrality and harmony are realized, heaven and earth
take their proper places and all things receive their full nourish-
ment.

Confucius said: The life of a Gentleman is an example of the
Mean, the life of an inferior man is a contradiction of it.

The life of a Gentleman is an example of the Mean, because
he is a Gentleman and holds to the centre. The inferior man's
life is a contradiction of the Mean, because he is an inferior man
and knows no restraint.

(Tzu Ssu, The Mean 1–2)

29. Five Human Relationships (Tzu Ssu)

Tzu Ssu also stated the Five Relationships which have served as a model of life in both China and Japan.

There are five relationships which concern all men, and three virtues by which they are fulfilled. The relationships of ruler and subject, father and son, husband and wife, older and younger brother, and relations between friends. These five are the relationships which belong to all men. Knowledge, humanity, and courage – these three are virtues which apply to all men, and that by which they are practised is one.

(*ibid. 20*)

30. The Path of Virtue (Dhammapada)

The Dhamma-pada, 'Virtue-path', is one of the oldest Buddhist texts, the earliest extant copy dating from the first century A.D., *and composed long before. It is a popular summary of morality which many people learn by heart. The Buddha taught a Middle Path, between extremes of sensuality and asceticism, and a Noble Eightfold Path of mental and moral discipline (see p. 18 above).*

The Eightfold Path is the best of paths, the Four Noble Truths are the best of truths, freedom from attachment is the best virtue, the seer is the best of men.

This is the path, there is no other that leads to purifying insight. Follow this path, that will confuse death.

Travelling on this path will end your suffering. It is the path that I preached when I learnt to throw off my bonds.

You yourself must strive, the blessed ones are only preachers.

Those who strive and meditate are freed from the bonds of death.

'All created things are passing'; when one sees and realizes this, he is superior to sorrow. This is the path to purity.

'All created things are sorrowful'; when one sees and realizes this, he is superior to sorrow. This is the path to purity.

'All the elements of being are not-self'; when one sees and realizes this, it is superior to sorrow. This is the path to purity.

He who fails to strive when it is time to strive, who though he is young and strong is lazy and irresolute, that idle man will not find the path to wisdom.

He who guards his speech, controls his mind, and does nothing wrong, keeping these three roads of action clear, he will achieve the path taught by the wise.

Wisdom springs from meditation, and from neglect of it the loss of wisdom. When he knows this path of progress or decline, a man should choose the path that leads to the growth of wisdom.

(Dhammapada 20, 1–10; 273–282)

31. Virtuous Conduct (Qur'an)

It is not virtuous conduct to turn your faces to the east or to the west. But virtuous conduct is that of those who believe in God, and the Last Day, and the angels, and the book, and the prophets. Those who, for the love of him bestow their wealth upon relatives, and orphans and the poor, upon the followers of the way, and beggars, and to ransom captives. Those who observe prayer and give alms. Those who keep a covenant when they have entered into one, who endure steadfastly under adversity and hardship, and during attacks. These are the ones who speak truth, these are the ones who show piety.

(Qur'an 2, 172/177)

32. No Extremes (Proverbs)

Two things I have asked of you, deny them not to me before I
die:
  Remove far from me vanity and lies;
  give me neither poverty nor riches;
feed me with the food that is needful for me.
  Lest I am full and deny you, and say, 'Who is the Lord?'
  or lest I am poor, and steal, and profane the name of my
God.

(Proverbs 30, 7–9)

33. Morality and Religion (Gandhi)

No work done by any man, however great, will really prosper
unless it has a distinct religious backing. But what is Religion? I
for one would answer: Not the Religion you will get after reading
all the scriptures of the world. Religion is not really what is
grasped by the brain, but a heart grasp.

Religion is not a thing alien to us. It has to be evolved out of
us. It is always within us: with some, consciously so; with others,
quite unconsciously. But it is always there. And whether we
wake up this religious instinct in us through outside assistance or
by inward growth, no matter how it is done, it has got to be done,
if we want to do anything in the right manner, or to achieve
anything that is going to persist.

(Mahatma Gandhi's Ideas, p. 101f.)

Discussion

Make a list of the virtues that seem best to you.

Compare the Five Virtues of Confucius with the Three Treasures of Taoism.

How were American Indian morality and virtue expressed?

Consider Aristotle's idea of Virtue as the Mean or Middle Way.

The Life of the Gentleman is an example of the Mean (Confucius). Discuss.

What is virtuous conduct?

Consider the Characters and Tempers described in the Mishnah.

III

SPECIAL VIRTUES

Every civilization has ideals which it prizes and which give it special character. Some particular virtues, and some secondary duties, are selected here.

34. Wisdom (Plato)

It has been seen (page 26) that Plato regarded wisdom as the supreme virtue, and a further passage illustrates his view of wisdom as inborn in every soul, and needing only the right direction or education to make it useful.

There is a faculty residing in the soul of each person, and an instrument enabling each of us to learn; and just as we might suppose it to be impossible to turn the eye round from darkness to light without turning the whole body, so must this faculty, or this instrument, be wheeled round, in company with the entire soul, from the perishing world, until it is enabled to endure the contemplation of the real world and the brightest part of it, which, according to us, is the Form of Good . . . Hence this very process of revolution must give rise to an art, teaching in what way the change will most easily and most effectually be brought about. Its object will not be to generate in the person the power of seeing. On the contrary, it assumes that he possesses it, though he is turned in a wrong direction, and does not look towards the right quarter; and its aim is to remedy this defect . . .

Hence, while on the one hand the other so-called virtues of the soul seem to resemble those of the body, inasmuch as they really do not pre-exist in the soul, but are formed in it in the course of time by habit and exercise; the virtue of Wisdom, on the other hand, does most certainly appertain, as it would appear, to a more divine substance which never loses its energy, but by change of position becomes useful and serviceable, or else remains useless and injurious.

(Republic 7, 518–9)

35. Friendship (Cicero)

Friendship has been written about in many societies and Cicero wrote a long essay on it.

I can only exhort you to look on Friendship as the most valuable of all human possessions, no other being equally suited to the moral nature of man, or so applicable to every state and circumstance, whether of prosperity or adversity, in which he can possibly be placed. But at the same time I lay it down as a fundamental axiom that 'true Friendship can only subsist between those who are animated by the strictest principles of honour and virtue'. . . .

In my opinion, therefore, whoever restrains his passions within the bounds of reason, and uniformly acts, in all the relations of life, upon one steady, consistent principle of approved honour, justice, and beneficence, that man is in reality, as well as in common estimation, strictly and truly good . . .

Friendship may be shortly defined, 'a perfect conformity of opinions upon all religious and civil subjects, united with the highest degree of mutual esteem and affection'.

(On Friendship)

36. Justice (Isaiah, Hosea)

The Hebrew concept of righteousness (Book I, 1) was extended by the prophets beyond religious rituals to social concerns, especially towards the oppressed.

Wash yourselves, make yourselves clean, put away the evil of your doings from before my eyes.

Cease to do evil, learn to do well.

Seek justice, relieve the oppressed, defend the fatherless, plead for the widow.

Come now, let us reason together, says the Lord: though your sins are like scarlet, they shall be as white as snow; though they are red like crimson, they shall become like wool.

(Isaiah 1, 16–18)

My judgement goes forth as the light, for I desire mercy and not sacrifice, and the knowledge of God rather than burnt offerings.

(Hosea 6, 5–6)

37. Whatever is True (Paul)

Whatsoever things are true, whatsoever things are honourable, whatsoever things are just, whatsoever things are pure, whatsoever things are lovely, whatsoever things are of good report; if there is any virtue, and if there is any praise, think about these things.

(Philippians 4, 8)

The fruit of the Spirit is love, joy, peace, patience, kindness, goodness, faithfulness, gentleness, self-control: against such there is no law.

(Galatians 5, 22–23)

38. Kindness (Qur'an)

Serve God, and do not associate any other with him.

Show kindness to parents, to relatives, orphans and the poor, to the person who is under your protection whether he is a relative or not, to the companion by your side, and to a follower of the way, and to those that your right hands possess. Truly, God does not love a conceited boaster.

Those who are miserly, and urge the people to miserliness, and hide the bounty which God has bestowed on them . . .

And those who spend their riches for display before the people, not believing in God and the Last Day . . .

What harm would it do them if they were to believe in God and the Last Day, and give away something of that which God has provided for them? God has come to know about them.

Truly God does no wrong, even to the weight of a grain; and if there is a good deed he doubles it, and he bestows from himself a great reward.

(Qur'an 4, 40–44)

39. Proper Work (Gita, third century B.C.)

The Indian concept of duty or right (see Book I, 2), applied to the different classes, gave each its special or proper duties and activities.

In patience, pureness, calm, control,
in uprightness, austerity,
in pure and practised wisdom, faith,
priests have their own activity.

In valour, firmness, majesty,
in lordly nature, charities,
in skill and courage in the fight,
are the warrior's own activities.

To plough and trade and tend the herds
for artisans are proper work,
and toil with service as its soul
that is a servant's proper work.

Delighting in his special work
a man may reach perfectedness,
hear how a man may win success
delighting in his special work.

For a man attains perfection
in special action worshipping
the One who permeates all this,
source of activity of being.

(Bhagavad Gita 18, 42–46)

40. Divine Qualities (Gita)

> Boldness and purity of heart,
> disciplined wisdom, steadfastness,
> restraint and study, prayers and alms,
> austerity and uprightness.
>
> Renouncing, without lies or wrath,
> at peace, with harmlessness and truth,
> modesty, no greed or fickleness,
> kindness to beings, gentleness.
>
> Ardour, patience, strength and cleanness,
> but lacking pride and lacking hate –
> such are the qualities of one
> who is born to the divine estate.
>
> *(Bhagavad Gita 16, 1–3)*

41. No Injury (Jain)

The Jain religion of India has laid special emphasis upon non-violence (a-himsa) to any creatures (see Book I, 53).

In whatever house or village or town or city a monk may be, if he is attacked by violent men or is subject to any hardship, he should bear it like a hero. A saint, with true understanding, has compassion for all the world, and knowing the sacred truth he should preach, spread and proclaim it in the east, west, south and north. He should proclaim it among those who exert themselves and those who do not, and among all who are willing to hear him.

Without neglecting tranquillity, detachment, patience, liberation, purity, uprightness, gentleness, and freedom from care, he should with due consideration preach the law of the monks to all kinds of creatures . . .

One should do no injury to oneself, nor to anybody else, nor to any of the different kinds of living beings.

But a great sage, neither injuring nor injured, becomes a shelter for all sorts of afflicted creatures, like an island that is never covered with water.

(Acharanga Sutra 1, 6, 5)

42. Righteousness (Dhammapada)

A man is not righteous who carries out his purpose by violence, but he is just who discriminates between right and wrong.

He who guides others with calm and equitable judgement is called a wise and righteous guardian of the law.

A man is not wise by much speaking. He is called wise who is calm, free from hatred and fear.

A man is not a pillar of the law by much speaking. He is called a pillar of the law who even hearing part of it does not neglect the law.

A man is not an elder simply because his hair is grey. Mere old age is called empty old age. He is called an elder in whom dwell truth, righteousness, non-violence, self-control and self-mastery, who is without taint and wise.

One does not become handsome by mere talk or comeliness, if one is envious, greedy and wicked. But he is called handsome in whom these faults are destroyed from the root, and who is wise and pure.

(Dhammapada 256–263)

43. **Truth** (Buddhist Dialogues)

For Buddhists the truth or doctrine (dharma) *is the refuge to which men go, along with the Buddha who made known the truth, and the Order which he founded. Here a king is speaking to the Buddha after being convinced of the truth of his teaching.*

Just as if a man were to set up that which has been thrown down, or were to reveal that which is hidden away, or were to point out the right road to him who has gone astray, or were to bring a lamp into the darkness so that those who have eyes could see external forms – just even so, Lord, has the truth been made known to me, in many a figure, by the Blessed One.

And now I betake myself, Lord, to the Blessed One as my refuge, to the Truth, and to the Order. May the Blessed One accept me as a disciple, as one who, from this day forth, as long as life endures, has taken his refuge in them.

Sin overcame me, Lord, weak and foolish and wrong that I am ... May the Blessed One accept it of me, Lord, that do so acknowledge it as a sin, to the end that in future I may restrain myself ...

Whosoever looks upon his fault as a fault, and rightfully confesses it, shall attain to self-restraint in the future.

(*Samanna-phala Sutta 85, in Digha Nikaya*)

44. **Humanity and Righteousness** (Mencius)

Mencius based his teachings on the principle of humanity (jen), like Confucius, and added to it the concept of righteousness or duty (i). He thought that virtues were innate in man but needed development.

Human nature will do good when it is left to follow its natural feelings, therefore I say it is good. If it becomes evil that is not the fault of its original nature. All men have a sense of mercy, all men have a sense of shame, all men have a sense of respect, all men have a sense of right and wrong. The sense of mercy forms humanity, the sense of shame forms righteousness, the sense of respect forms decorum and the sense of right and wrong forms wisdom. Humanity, righteousness, decorum and wisdom are not introduced into us from outside; they are inherent in our nature, only we ignore them. So it is said, 'If you seek them you will find them, but if you neglect them you will lose them.' Some men have these virtues much more than others, twice as much, or five times, or far more, and that is because the others have not developed their original capacities to their full extent.

(Mencius 6, A 6)

45. **Simplicity** (Tao Te Ching)

The Tao Te Ching attacks formal virtues and artificial morality, and suggests the symbol of the Uncarved Block as the unity and purity beneath the complexity of life.

Cast off wisdom, discard knowledge, and the people will benefit a hundredfold. Get rid of benevolence, discard morality, and the people will return to filial piety. Banish scheming, discard gain, and thieves and robbers will disappear. These three precepts are not enough, and people must have something to look at. Show them Simplicity, give them the Uncarved Block, to reduce selfishness and to moderate desires.

(Tao Te Ching 19)

Discussion

Wisdom appertains to a divine substance (Plato). Discuss.
Is Friendship the most valuable of human possessions?
Compare justice (Isaiah) with kindness (Qur'an).
What is a man's special work?
Consider the Jain doctrine of non-violence.
All men have a sense of mercy (Mencius). Do you agree?
Discard morality. What does the Tao Te Ching mean by this?

IV

HAPPINESS

*Happiness has often been taken as the chief, or one of the chief,
of the goals of life. But what kind of happiness, and what its
relationship is to pleasure, has been much disputed. Aristotle
began his Ethics with a discussion of the nature of Happiness.*

46. Happiness and the Chief Good (Aristotle)

Since all knowledge and moral choice grasps at good of some kind
or another, what good is that which we say 'politics' [social
teaching] aims at? Or in other words, what is the highest of all
the goods which are the objects of action? So far as the name
goes, there is pretty general agreement, for both the multitude
and the refined few call it Happiness, and 'living well' and 'doing
well' they consider to be the same as 'being happy'. But about
the Nature of this Happiness men dispute, and the multitude do
not agree with the wise in their account of it.

For some say it is one of those things which are palpable and
apparent, like pleasure or wealth or honour. In fact some say one
thing and some another, indeed often the same man gives a
different account of it. For when he is ill he calls it health, when
poor he calls it wealth. And conscious of their own ignorance,
men admire those who talk grandly and above their com-
prehension. Some again hold it to be something by itself,
different from and beside these many good things, which is in
fact the cause of their being good . . . Now of the Chief Good
[namely, of Happiness] men seem to form their notions from
their different ways of life, as we might expect. Many and the
lowest think it is pleasure, and so they are content with a life of

52

sensual enjoyment. For there are three lines of life which stand out prominently to view: the one just mentioned, and then life in society, and thirdly the life of contemplation . . .

We always choose Happiness for its own sake, and never with a view to something further. Whereas honour, pleasure, intellect, and every excellence . . . we choose also with a view to happiness, thinking that through their agency we shall be happy. But no man chooses Happiness with a view to these things, nor in fact with a view to any other thing whatever . . . So then Happiness is manifestly something final and self-sufficient, being the end of all things which are and may be done.

(Ethics 1, 4, 7)

47. Desire and Wisdom (Plato)

He who has always been occupied with the cravings of desire and ambition, and who interests himself wholly in it, will of necessity have got all his notions mortal. And as far as possible he will become altogether mortal; nor will he fall short of this in any way, since he has cherished his mortal part.

But he who has earnestly striven after learning and true wisdom, and has been fully trained and exercised in it, if he lays hold of the truth must of necessity acquire an immortal and heavenly temper. Indeed, as far as human nature is capable of it, he will in no way fall short of immortality. And since he is serving the divine, and has the genius which dwells in him ordered aright, he must be exceedingly blessed.

(Timaeus, 90)

53

48. Happiness, Knowledge and Action (Marcus Aurelius, A.D. 121–180)

Herein consists happiness of life, for a man to know thoroughly the true nature of everything, what is its matter and what is its form; and with all his heart and soul to do always that which is just, and speak the truth. What remains then but to enjoy your life in a course and coherence of good actions, one succeeding immediately upon another, and never interrupted even for a little while . . .

What do you desire? To live long. Why? To enjoy the working of a sensitive soul, or of the appetites? Or would you grow, and then decrease again? Would you be able to talk for long, and think and reason with yourself? Which of all these things seems to be a worthy object of your desire? Now if you find that all of these are worth little in themselves, then proceed on to the last, which is in all things to follow God and reason.

(Meditations 12, 22–24)

49. Happy are they (Jesus)

Most translations keep the traditional 'blessed' for the description given by Jesus of those who are truly happy, and these verses are called the Beatitudes, 'blessings', though the original Greek word meant both blessed and happy. 'Poor in spirit' means both materially poor and spiritually dependent upon God, and the New English Bible translates it as 'those who know their need of God'.

Happy are the poor in spirit, for theirs is the kingdom of heaven.

Happy are those who mourn, for they shall be comforted.

Happy are the meek, for they shall inherit the earth.

Happy are those who hunger and thirst after righteousness, for they shall be filled.

Happy are the merciful, for they shall obtain mercy.

Happy are the pure in heart, for they shall see God.

Happy are the peacemakers, for they shall be called sons of God.

Happy are those who are persecuted for righteousness' sake, for theirs is the kingdom of heaven.

You are happy when men revile you and persecute you and utter all kinds of evil against you falsely for my sake. Rejoice and be glad, for your reward is great in heaven, for so men persecuted the prophets who were before you.

(Matthew 5, 3–12)

50. Joy and Peace (Paul)

Paul writes from prison to encourage his friends at Philippi.

Work out your own salvation with fear and trembling, for it is God who works in you both to will and to work for his good pleasure.

Do all things without murmuring and disputing, that you may be blameless and harmless, children of God without blemish in the midst of a crooked and perverse generation, among whom you shine as lights in the world, holding fast the word of life . . .

And if I am to be poured out upon the sacrificial offering of your faith, I am glad and rejoice with you all. And in the same manner you also should be glad and rejoice with me . . .

Rejoice in the Lord always; I say again, Rejoice.

Let all men know your forbearance. The Lord is at hand. Be anxious for nothing, but in everything by prayer and supplication, with thanksgiving, let your requests be made known to God. And the peace of God, which passes all understanding, will guard your hearts and minds in Christ Jesus . . .

Do the things which you learned and received and heard and saw in me, and the God of peace will be with you.

(Philippians 2, 12–18; 4, 4–9)

55

51. Divine Care (Qur'an)

Muhammad's father died before he was born, his mother when he was six and his grandfather when he was eight. The orphan childhood brought sadness but also the conviction of the providence of God.

By the morning brightness,
by the night stillness,
your Lord has not taken leave of you,
or despised you.
The end will be better for you than the beginning,
surely in the end the Lord will give you satisfaction.

Did he not find you an orphan and give you shelter?
Did he not find you wandering and guide you?
Did he not find you poor and enrich you?

So, as for the orphan, be not harsh,
As for the beggar, do not scold him,
And as for the goodness of your Lord, talk about it.

(Qur'an 93)

52. Happiness and Peace (Upanishads)

The Inner Soul of all beings,
the One Controller makes his one form manifold –
the wise who perceive him as abiding in themselves,
they and no others have eternal happiness.

He is permanent among the impermanent,
intelligent among intelligences,
the One among many, who grants desires –
the wise who perceive him as abiding in themselves,
they and no others have eternal peace.

This is it, they recognize,
the highest, indescribable happiness . . .
After Him, as He shines, everything shines,
this whole world is illuminated with His light.

(Katha Upanishad 5, 12–15)

53. **We live happily** (Dhammapada)

We live happily, hating no one in the midst of men who
hate.
Let us indeed dwell free from hatred among men who hate.

We live happily, healthy among those who are diseased.
Let us indeed dwell free from disease among men who are
sick.

We live happily, free from care among those who are care-
worn.
Let us indeed dwell without care among men who are care-
worn.

We live happily, possessing nothing.
Let us dwell, feeding on happiness, like the shining gods.

Victory breeds hatred, the conquered sleeps in sorrow.
The man is calm who has given up both victory and defeat.

There is no fire like lust, no evil like hatred,
no sorrow like existence, no happiness greater than
tranquillity.

(Dhammapada 197–202)

57

54. Wealth and the Way (Confucius)

Wealth and rank are what every man desires, but if they can only be obtained by transgressing the right Way, they must be abandoned. Poverty and obscurity are what every man detests, but if they can be avoided only by transgressing the right Way, they must be accepted. If a gentleman forsakes Goodness, how can he bear that name? A gentleman never leaves the way of Goodness, even for a single meal. In moments of haste, he cleaves to it; in times of danger, he cleaves to it.

The Master said: I have never seen one who really loved Goodness, nor one who really hated wickedness. One who really loved Goodness, would not prize anything above it. And one who really hated wickedness, would do Good so constantly that wickedness would never cling to him. Is anyone ever able to do Good, with all his might, for a single day? Yet I have never seen anyone give up the attempt because he had not the strength to go on.

(Analects 4, 5–6)

55. Quietness (Tao Te Ching)

Push far towards the Void, hold fast to Quietness, and the ten
thousand creatures can be worked on by you.
I have seen their return.
See how all return to the roots from which they grew.
Returning to the root is known as Quietness.
That is what is meant by submission to Fate,
submission to Fate is known as the constant,
to know the constant is to be enlightened.
Not to know it means disaster.
He who knows the constant has room for everything,
he who has room for everything is without prejudice.
To be without prejudice is kingly,
to be kingly is of heaven,
to be of heaven is to be in the Way.
The Way is forever and he that possesses it
is not destroyed when his body ceases to be.

(Tao Te Ching 16)

Discussion

What is your idea of happiness?
Consider the happiness of those who are merciful.
Work out your own salvation, for God works in you. Explain.
We always choose happiness for its own sake (Aristotle).
Discuss.
We live happily among men who hate. How?
If a Gentleman forsakes goodness, how can he bear that
name?
What do you desire?

V

UNSELFISH ACTION

There is widespread belief that action should not be undertaken simply for personal gain, and indeed that such a motive is against the best interests of the individual and of society. Behaviour should be unselfish. The ancient Hindu Laws of Manu recognize the difficulty of this ideal.

56. The Impulse of Desire (Manu)

To act solely from a desire for rewards is not praiseworthy yet freedom from that desire is not found in this world . . .

The desire for rewards indeed has its root in the notion that an act can yield them, and through that idea sacrifices are performed. Vows and laws prescribing restraints are all stated to be kept through the idea that they will bear fruit.

Not a single act here below ever appears to be done by a man free from desire; for whatever a man does it is the result of the impulse of desire.

He who persists in discharging his duties in the right way, reaches the deathless state, and even in this life he obtains the fulfilment of all the desires he may have held.

(Manu 2, 2–5)

57. **Disciplined Action** (Gita)

The Bhagavad Gita goes into the question of behaviour much more thoroughly. It insists that man must act, and that to renounce physical acts is useless because the mind will still dwell on sensual things. So mind and body must be controlled, action is better than inaction, but it must be done without attachment to results. The best men must act also as an example to others, as God himself acts to support the world and help man. This disciplined activity is called Yoga.

A man does not win freedom from works by not doing them, and not by mere renunciation can he win perfection.

No one, even for a moment, can remain without any action, for every man is caused to act by the powers of nature.

One who restrains his limbs from action, but sits with his mind pondering sensual things, is called a hypocrite.

But he is more excellent who controls his senses with his mind, and with his limbs undertakes disciplined action in detachment.

You must do your duty, for work is better than no work, and even the maintenance of the body cannot succeed without work.

So work to this end, but free from attachment to rewards ...

Whatever the noblest man does, other people will do also, and what he makes his standard the world will follow ... If I [the deity] did not continue working tirelessly men everywhere would follow my path.

If I did not do my work these worlds would perish, and I should be a worker of confusion and destroy these creatures.

Foolish men act attached to their work, but the wise should act in detachment, to bring about the welfare of the world.

The wise man should not bring confusion to the ignorant who are attached to action, he should let them enjoy all their actions, but himself act with discipline.

(Gita 3, 4–8, 21–26)

58. Only for the Soul (Upanishads)

*Two identical passages in the Upanishads state that the real motive
of action is the soul. This is not self-love, but concern for the inner
reality, the true soul, which is the most precious element in all beings.
A wife is asking her philosopher husband how to find immortality.*

If this whole earth with its wealth were mine, would I be
immortal with that?

No, he said, As the life of the rich, so would your life be. But
there is no hope of immortality through wealth ... Come, sit
down, let me explain it to you. And while I am talking do you
meditate upon it.

Then he said: Truly, not for love of the husband is a husband
dear, but for love of the soul a husband is dear.

Truly, not for love of the wife is a wife dear, but for love of the
soul a wife is dear ...

Truly, it is the soul that should be seen, listened to, thought
about, pondered on. Truly, with seeing, listening, thinking and
understanding the soul all this world is known.

(Brihad-aranyaka Upanishad 2, 4, 2–5; 4, 5, 3–6)

59. Not to be Seen (Jesus)

*The Gospel prescribes religious duties, but directed towards God and
not to get credit for piety from men.*

Take heed not to do your righteousness before men, to be seen
by them, otherwise you will have no reward from your Father
who is in heaven.

Therefore, when you give alms, sound no trumpet before you,
as the hypocrites do in the synagogues and in the streets, that
they may have glory from men. Truly, I tell you, they have their
reward. But when you give alms, do not let your left hand know
what your right hand is doing, so that your alms may be in secret,
and your Father who sees in secret will reward you.

And when you pray, you must not be like the hypocrites, for they love to stand and pray in the synagogues and at the street corners, that they may be seen by men. Truly, I tell you, they have their reward. But when you pray, go into your room and shut the door and pray to your Father who is in secret; and your Father who sees in secret will reward you . . .

And when you fast, do not look sad, like the hypocrites, for they disfigure their faces that they may be seen by men. Truly, I tell you, they have their reward. But when you fast, anoint your head and wash your face, that your fasting may not be seen by men; and your Father who sees in secret will reward you.

(Matthew 6, 1–6, 16–18)

60. The Least of These (Jesus)

Then the king will say to those at his right hand, Come, O blessed of my Father, inherit the kingdom prepared for you from the foundation of the world. For I was hungry and you gave me food, I was thirsty and you gave me drink, I was a stranger and you took me in, I was naked and you clothed me, I was ill and you visited me, I was in prison and you came to me.

Then the righteous will answer him, Lord, when did we see you hungry and feed you, or thirsty and give you drink?

When did we see you a stranger and took you in, or naked and clothed you? When did we see you ill or in prison and visited you?

And the king will answer them, Truly, I say to you, as you did it to one of the least of these my brothers you did it to me.

(Matthew 25, 34–40)

61. Genuine Love (Paul)

Let love be genuine. Hate what is evil, hold to what is good.
Love one another with brotherly affection, preferring one
another in honour. Do not fail in zeal, but be fervent in spirit and
serve the Lord. Rejoice in hope, be patient in suffering, continue
in prayer. Contribute to the needs of believers, and practise
hospitality.

Bless those who persecute you, bless them and do not curse
them. Rejoice with those who rejoice, and weep with those who
weep. Have the same mind towards one another. Do not be
proud, but associate with the lowly, and be not conceited.

Repay no one evil for evil, but take thought for what is
honourable in the sight of all. If possible, as far as it depends on
you, live in peace with all men.

Beloved do not avenge yourselves, but leave it to divine retribution, for it is written, Justice is mine, I will repay, says the
Lord. But if your enemy is hungry, feed him. If he is thirsty, give
him drink. For in doing so you will heap live coals on his head.
Do not be overcome by evil, but overcome evil with good.

(Romans 12, 9–21)

62. Not Fear but Love (Rabi'a)

One day a number of saints saw that Rabi'a had taken fire in one
hand and water in the other and was running with speed. They
said to her, O lady of the next world, where are you going and
what is the meaning of this?

She said: I am going to light fire in Paradise and to pour water
on to Hell, so that both veils [i.e. hindrances to the true vision of
God] may completely disappear from the pilgrims and their
purpose may be sure, and the servants of God may see him,
without any object of hope or motive of fear . . .

Again she used to pray:

O my Lord, If I worship thee from fear of Hell, burn me in Hell, and if I worship thee from hope of Paradise, exclude me thence, but if I worship thee for thine own sake then withhold not from me thine eternal Beauty.

(Rabi'a the Mystic, pp. 98f., 30)

63. Not for Heaven or Hell (Xavier)

Francis Xavier (1506–1552) was a Jesuit missionary to Asia. This hymn attributed to him may be a rendering of a Spanish sonnet.

My God, I love thee – not because
    I hope for heaven thereby,
Nor yet because who love thee not
    Are lost eternally.

Not with the hope of gaining aught,
    Not seeking a reward,
But as thyself hast loved me
    O ever-loving Lord.

E'en so I love thee, and will love,
    And in thy praise will sing,
Because thou art my loving God
    And my eternal King.

(trs. E. Caswall, 1849)

64. Actionless Activity (Tao Te Ching)

The Chinese Taoists thought that being free from desire even a ruler could be filled with such power that his subjects would turn from their evil desires. So by actionless activity (wu wei) and silent teaching all creatures would be affected.

The wise man relies on actionless activity and teaches without words. But he works upon the ten thousand creatures and does not disown them.

He gives them life but does not claim possession.

He controls them but does not oppress them.

He fulfils his aim but does not call himself a victor.

And because he does not call himself a victor, he never loses the fruits of what he had done.

(Tao Te Ching 2)

65. The Perfect Way (Seng-t'san)

Zen Buddhism emphasizes 'meditation' (Zen in Japanese, Ch'an in Chinese, from Indian Dhyana). This meditation tries to see behind the elements of the world the truth beyond, and knowledge of it brings enlightenment. This passage is from a Chinese teacher of the seventh century A.D.

The Perfect Way knows no difficulties
except that it refuses to make preferences;
only when freed from hate and desire
it reveals itself fully and without disguise.

A tenth of an inch's difference
and heaven and earth are set apart;
if you wish to see it before your own eyes
have no fixed thoughts either for or against it.

To set up what you like against what you dislike –
this is the disease of the mind;
when the deep meaning (of the Way) is not understood
peace of mind is disturbed to no purpose.
(Seng-t'san, trs. D. T. Suzuki, Manual of Zen Buddhism,
p. 76f.)

66. False Motivation (Tenri-kyo)

Tenri-kyo, the Religion of Divine Reason, founded by a peasant woman Miki (1798–1887) is one of the powerful new religions of Japan. In addition to its temples and rituals, Tenri-kyo lays great emphasis upon communal work under the guidance of the divine parent.

Although one divine parent is shared by all mankind, human beings, not knowing this truth, fail to understand that all others are equally brothers and sisters who are the children of the divine parent. Thus, motivated by the false notion that each one lives only for his own sake, they tend to live with self-centred thinking and selfish actions, which harm and cloud others' minds and disrupt the harmony of the world . . .

Preoccupied by their own suffering, happiness and profit, human beings often think contrary to the will of (the divine parent) who wishes the harmony and happiness of all mankind. The divine parent warns men against such selfish concern by using the analogy of dust (which can easily accumulate and clouds our minds). He cautions us to reflect on the eight kinds of mental dust – vindictiveness, possessiveness, hatred, self-centredness, enmity, anger, greed, and arrogance. The important thing for all of us to realize is that we have borrowed our life and that it is (the divine parent who had lent it to us), and do not neglect the daily dusting of our minds.

(Doctrinal Manual of Tenri-kyo, p. 57, trs. J. M. Kitagawa, The Great Asian Religions, p. 303)

67. Unto this Last (Ruskin)

John Ruskin (1819–1900) wrote on art and economics, teaching the true nature of wealth and the need for just wages. The title of the essay quoted here was taken from a parable of Jesus (Matthew 20, 14).

All true economy is 'Law of the house'. Strive to make that law strict, simple, generous: waste nothing, and grudge nothing. Care in nowise to make more of money, but care to make much of it; remembering always the great, palpable, inevitable fact – the rule and root of all economy – that what one person has, another cannot have; and that every atom of substance, of whatever kind, used or consumed, is so much human life spent: which, if it issue in the saving present life, or gaining more, is well spent, but if not is either so much life prevented, or so much slain . . .

Luxury is indeed possible in the future – innocent and exquisite; luxury for all, and by the help of all; but luxury at present can only be enjoyed by the ignorant: the cruellest man living could not sit at his feast, unless he sat blindfold. Raise the veil boldly; face the light; and if, as yet, the light of the eye can only be through tears, and the light of the body through sackcloth, go thou forth weeping, bearing precious seed, until the time come, and the kingdom, when Christ's gift of bread, and bequest of peace, shall be 'Unto this last as unto thee'.

(Unto this Last, Ad Valorem)

Discussion

To act from a desire for rewards is not praiseworthy. Why?

For love of the soul a husband (or wife) is dear. Discuss.

They pray to be seen of men; they have their reward. What is it?

What is actionless activity?

Luxury at present can only be enjoyed by the ignorant. Discuss.

No one can remain without doing any action. Consider this.

Reflect on the kinds of mental dust.

VI

WRONGDOING

Notions of wrongdoing, vice and wickedness, reflect their opposite, the ideals of right which vary with different traditions. That evil is an absence of good, an ignorance of knowledge, was an attractive theory, but it did not seem to fit all the facts. Socrates thought that the essence of virtue was intelligence, and therefore the essence of vice must be ignorance. He uttered the celebrated paradox, 'no man sins unwillingly'. Yet men do so, and Aristotle showed that passion could carry man away beyond his knowledge and will.

68. Choice of Evil (Aristotle)

Virtue is in our power. So too is Vice. Because wherever it is in our power to act, it is also in our power not to act, and the reverse ... But if it is in our power to do and to forbear doing what is creditable or the contrary, and these respectively constitute being good or bad, then being good or vicious characters is in our power.

As for the well-known saying, 'No man is voluntarily wicked or involuntarily happy', it is partly true and partly false. For no man is happy against his will, of course, but wickedness is voluntary ...

Furthermore, it is wholly irrelevant to say that the man who acts unjustly or dissolutely does not wish to attain the habits of these vices: for if a man wittingly does those things whereby he must become unjust, he is to all intents and purposes unjust voluntarily.

(Ethics 3, 5)

It is a strange thing, as Socrates thought, that while knowledge is present in his mind something else should master him and drag him about like a slave. Socrates in fact contended against the theory, maintaining that there is no such state as that of imperfect self-control, for no one acts contrary to what is best, conceiving it to be best by reason of ignorance of what is best.

With all due respect to Socrates, his account of the matter is at variance with plain facts, and we must inquire with respect to the feeling, and if it is caused by ignorance then what is the nature of the ignorance. For that the man so failing does not suppose his acts to be right before he is under the influence of passion is quite plain.

(Ethics 7, 2)

69. The Fool (Psalms)

In the Bible wrongdoing is regarded not only as an offence against man but against God and is a sin. The meanings of this term vary, from deviation from the right way, to rebellion against God which brings a changed relationship until it is set right. Yet wrong is sometimes seen as human folly and lack of knowledge.

> The fool has said in his heart, There is no God.
> They are corrupt, they do abominable works,
> there is none that does good.
> The Lord looks down from heaven upon the children of men, to see if there are any that understand, that seek after God.
> They have all gone astray, they are all alike corrupt;
> there is none that does good, no, not one.
> Have all the workers of evil no knowledge,
> who eat up my people as they eat bread,
> and do not call on the Lord?
> There they shall be in great fear,
> for God is with the generation of the righteous.
> You put to shame the counsels of the poor
> but the Lord is his refuge.

(Psalm 14, 1–6)

70. Not what I want (Paul)

Paul saw a power of evil that led him away from his good resolutions and knowledge.

I do not understand what I am doing. For I do not do what I want, but I do what I hate. But if I do what I do not want, I agree that the law is good. So it is no longer I that act, but sin which dwells in me. For I know that nothing good dwells in me, that is, in my flesh. For I have the will, but not the power to do good. I do not do the good that I want, but I do the evil that I do not want. But if I do what I do not want, it is no more I that do it, but sin which dwells in me.

I find then a law that when I want to do good, evil is with me. For I delight in the law of God in my inner self, but I see a different law in the members of my body, warring against the law of my mind, and making me captive to the law of sin which is in my members.

Wretched man that I am, who will deliver me from this body doomed to death? God will, through Jesus Christ our Lord!

(Romans 7, 15–25)

71. Vices (Paul)

The works of the flesh are plain: immorality, impurity, indecency; idolatry and sorcery; quarrels, strife, jealousy, anger, selfishness, dissension, party intrigues and envy; drunkenness, orgies, and the like. I warn you, as I warned you before, that those who do such things will not inherit the kingdom of God.

The divine retribution is revealed from heaven against all ungodliness and unrighteousness of men, who hold down the truth in unrighteousness.

Because that which may be known about God is plain to them, for God has shown it to them. Ever since the creation of the world his invisible nature, namely his eternal power and deity, has been clearly seen, being perceived in the things that are made.

So they are without excuse; because although they knew God they did not honour him as God or gave thanks to him. But they became vain in their thinking, and their senseless minds were darkened. Claiming to be wise, they became fools. And they exchanged the glory of the immortal God for images of mortal man or birds or animals or reptiles.

Therefore God gave them up in the lusts of their hearts to impurity, to dishonouring their bodies among themselves. Because they exchanged the truth of God for a lie, and worshipped and served the creature rather than the Creator who is blessed forever.

(Galatians 5, 19–21; Romans 1, 18–25)

72. Association (Qur'an)

For Islam the worst sin is 'association' (shirk), the joining of false gods to the one true God, as practised by polytheists.

God will not forgive the association of anything with himself, although he forgives anything short of that to whoever he wishes. He who associates anything with God has strayed far into error . . .

To God belongs whoever is in heaven and earth. Those who are with him are not too proud for his service, nor are they wearied. They praise him day and night without fail.

Have men chosen gods who rise up from the earth? If there were any gods in heaven and earth except God, they would both go to ruin. So glory be to God, Lord of the throne, away from what they say. He will not be questioned about what he does, but they will be questioned.

(Qur'an 4, 116; 21, 19–23)

73. **Rich Fool** (Gita)

'Look this is what I gained today
and this desire I shall obtain,
for this is mine and also mine
is any wealth that comes again.

'Yes, yonder enemy I slew
and I shall slaughter others too;
I am the lord and joys belong
to me as perfect, happy, strong.

'See, I am rich, of noble line,
and whose can be compared to mine?
Since I shall give, rejoice and pray' –
So, fooled by ignorance, they say.

(*Bhagavad Gita 16, 13–15*)

74. **Against his Will** (Gita)

The Gita also sees that, despite knowledge and will power, there comes the force of passion, which destroys wisdom, and this must be controlled by self-discipline.

By what means incited on
does any man commit a sin?
Even moved against his will
as driven by a force within?

This is lust and this is anger,
derived from Passion's quality;
all-consuming, very wicked,
so know it here as enemy.

Therefore you must at once begin
to bring the senses into discipline,
while striking down this thing of ills
which pure and practical wisdom kills.

(*Bhagavad Gita 3, 36–37; 3, 41*)

75. Craving (Dhammapada)

Classical Buddhist teaching saw the source of all human misery in craving or desire, and its presence and cure was expressed in the Four Noble Truths and the Noble Eightfold Path (see page 18).

The craving of a thoughtless man spreads like a creeper.

He leaps from birth to birth, like a monkey seeking fruit.

Whoever is subdued by this fierce poisonous craving in this world, his sorrows increase more and more like abounding grass after rain.

But whoever overcomes this fierce and powerful craving in this world, sorrows fall away from him like water off a lotus leaf.

I give you this good counsel, all who are gathered here: dig up the roots of craving as one digs up the abounding grass to find the fragrant root, so that death may not destroy you again and again as a river breaks the rushes.

(Dhammapada 334–337)

76. Injury to Beings (Jain)

For the sake of the splendour, honour and glory of this life; for the sake of birth, death and final liberation, for the removal of pain, man acts sinfully towards the earth, or causes others to act so, or allows others to act so. This deprives him of happiness and perfect wisdom . . .

He who injures earthly bodies does not understand and renounce the sinful acts. He who does not injure them, understands and renounces the sinful acts. Knowing them, a wise man should not act sinfully towards the earth, nor cause others to act so, nor allow others to act so.

He who knows these causes of sin relating to the earth, is called a reward-knowing sage.

(Acharanga Sutra I, I, 2)

77. **That is why** (Tao Te Ching)

In accordance with its naturalistic philosophy Taoism sees trouble coming from unnatural practices, the people are oppressed, yet paradoxically this helps them because they are less attached to life than their rulers.

The people are hungry, because those who rule them eat too much in taxes. That is why they are hungry.

The people are difficult to govern, because their rulers interfere with them. That is why they are difficult to govern.

The people take death lightly, because their rulers pursue life too much. That is why they take death lightly. But it is because they are not intent on life that they are superior to those who are intent on life.

(Tao Te Ching 75)

Discussion

Consider the views of Socrates and Aristotle on voluntary wrongdoing.

I do what I hate (Paul). Sinning against his will (Gita). Compare.

Make a list of vices.

Describe the rich fool.

Is craving (desire) the source of all misery?

Why are people difficult to govern?

Can you distinguish between sin and crime?

Time Chart of authors quoted in the four parts of this series

Before 10th c. B.C.			
	Moses	Vedas	Hammurabi
8th	Amos, Hosea Micah, Isaiah	Upanishads	
7th	Deuteronomy Leviticus	Jains	Zarathushtra
6th	Jeremiah	Buddha	Confucius
5th	Socrates		Mo Tzu Tzu Ssu
4th	Plato	Magi Manu	Mencius
	Aristotle Epicurus	Mahabharata	
3rd	Proverbs Song of Songs Job	Gita Ashoka Kautilya	Tao Te Ching Chuang Tzu Hsun Tzu
2nd		Lotus Dhammapada	Huai-nan Tzu
1st		Cicero Lucretius	Tung Chung-shu
A.D.			
1st	Jesus Paul, John Peter Josephus	Epictetus	Patanjali Milinda
2nd	Clement Diognetus	Mishnah Marcus A.	Kama Sutra
3rd		Plotinus	
4th		Sankhya	Fa-hsien
5th	Augustine		
6th		Shanti-Deva	Shotoku
7th		Muhammad	Seng-t'san

8th		Traditions	Nihongi
		Rabi'a	
9th		Hallaj	
10th		Ash'ari	Manikka
11th	Anselm	Khayyam	Chou Tun-yi
12th	Francis		Hemachandra
13th	Aquinas, Dante	Rumi	Nichiren
	Eckhart		
14th	Lollards	Battuta	
15th	Kempis		Kabir
	Machiavelli		Nanak
16th	More, Xavier		Amar Das, Arjan
	Shakespeare		Tulsidas, Mirabai
	Montaigne		
17th	Descartes, Pascal		Tukaram
	Spinoza, Andrewes		Aurangzeb
	Barclay, Penn, Guyon		Nakae
	Milton, Traherne		Yamaga Soko
18th	Paine, Jefferson		
	Hume, Kant, Newton		
	Berkeley, Rousseau, Wesley		
	Wordsworth, Coleridge, Shelley		
19th	Mill, Ruskin, Morris		Baha'u'llah
	Marx, Engels, Tolstoy		Abdu'l Baha
	James, Greenwell,		Miki
	Spencer and Gillen		
	Catlin, Morgan, Maning		
20th	Freud, Frazer, Buber	Aurobindo, Tagore, Iqbal	
	Huxley, Hammarskjold	Gandhi,	
	Teilhard, Solzhenitsyn	Mao	
	Firth, Beauvoir	Radhakrishnan	
		Kamal, Hussein	

PH. 3. PAR